JOHN MURPHY

Think CHANGE

Adapt and thrive, or fall behind.

Proactive leaders think change by recognizing that "change" challenges people to grow and adapt, or be swept aside as complacent and obsolete. To compete in the world today, we must strive to be different. We must expand our knowledge, sharpen our skills, and manage our time more effectively.

Change is not something to fear or resist. It is a blessing. It is the essence of life itself. By embracing and promoting positive change, we learn more about who we are and what we can do. We grow. We gain confidence. We make a difference by improving ourselves and enriching the world around us. With change, we are given the chance to turn today's pains into tomorrow's gains.

GRAPHICS BY BALANCE DESIGN

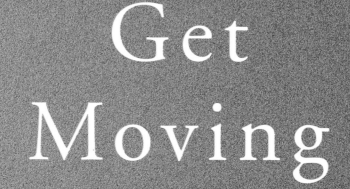

Get
Moving

Motivation means movement. It means tapping the power that lies within each one of us to move forward, to make a difference, to advance ourselves and the people around us. Motivation means going places and doing things, not standing still. When we focus our attention on change, innovation, growth, improvement, education, experimentation, adventure and discovery, we energize and enrich ourselves. We create momentum, a powerful force that provides confidence and self-esteem.

However, when we focus our attention on staying the same, on maintaining a fixed position, we start losing energy and suddenly find ourselves stagnant, outdated, and unmarketable. Soon, we are living in fear, doubting our abilities and overwhelmed with the rapidly changing world around us. We are fighting for the illusion of security, failing to recognize that real security lies within us.

It doesn't take a miracle to change. All it takes is a little faith, a willingness to trust yourself and a commitment to try something new. Anyone can do it, and everyone should. Make an effort to expand your horizons. Open your mind. Broaden your scope. The world is changing at an accelerating pace. Your choice is simple. Adapt and thrive, or fall behind.

Is your focus on growth and adventure or simply on staying the same? Are you willing to try something new?

One of the questions I like to ask in seminars and workshops is, "How many of you agree with the statement, 'Most people naturally resist change'?" The answer might surprise you. On average, 80-90% agree with the statement, suggesting that the majority of people perceive change negatively! Now consider the question yourself.

A quick look at human nature reveals worthwhile insights. Do people naturally grow older, or do we have to work at this? Is changing our minds and moods natural, or do we have to force these changes? Do our bodies change by themselves, or do we have to tell our cells what to do? Is variety the spice of life, or the enemy?

When we stop and evaluate the facts, one thing is certain. People are designed to change. We are engineered to grow, to expand beyond today; physically, mentally, emotionally and spiritually. The moment we lose sight of this, the instant we convince ourselves that change is bad, we begin limiting ourselves. Every age has its advantages, every outcome its silver linings. Those who learn to embrace change with optimism and enthusiasm prosper and endure. Those who attempt to fight what is natural fall behind. Do yourself a favor. Learn to adapt to our ever-changing environment and capitalize on your natural ability to change.

Do you believe that we are designed to change? Do you naturally resist change?

Adapt
and Grow

Eliminate Waste

Stop for a moment and define the "waste" in your life. Think about how you spend your time, talents, energy and resources. Do you find yourself getting caught up in unimportant matters, working hard but getting nowhere.

What about your physical, mental and emotional well-being? Are you dedicating time each day to your overall health? How about your talents and abilities? Are you realizing your full potential? What about the unlimited resources within your reach, the books, the libraries, the internet, the people, the products, the classes, the materials, the extraordinary amount of help available to you. Are you tapping into it?

Most people never recognize that the real enemy in life is our own inability to sort through the clutter and realize our full potential. Waste costs us time, opportunity and money. It costs us dignity and self-respect. It weighs us down. We know we can do better. We just don't. We accept waste as a normal part of life. It's easier to buy extra and throw some away. In many cases, we don't even keep track of it. It's easier to have someone else deal with it.

Don't waste the potential you have to shine! Think change! Declutter your life. Get your priorities straight. Put yourself to good use. You were born to give, not take. Eliminate the waste in your life and empower yourself to reach levels you may never have dreamed possible.

Are you organizing each day so that your most important priorities are tended to? And what about your ideas, your dreams and your suggestions? Are they going to waste?

Many times, the only way to achieve a vision of pleasure is by going through a period of pain and sacrifice. You want more income? You want higher margins? You want more energy? You want more knowledge? You want more time off? You want more security? You want better results? These images of pleasure often exist on the other side of pain and self-discipline. To get one, we have to experience the other. We have to give to get. Freedom and responsibility are two sides of the same coin.

So, what do you focus on? The pain or the pleasure? Do you approach life with optimism and enthusiasm, seeing past the pain? Or do you dwell on the dark side, denying yourself energy from within? Are you an agent of change or a victim of change? Choose your focus and you choose your energy level and your ultimate results.

Effective people see past the pain, focusing on the positive outcomes desired. When there is a problem, the winner is looking for solutions. When there is a mistake, the winner is looking for lessons to be learned. When there is a loss, the winner is searching for a gain. Highly effective people recognize that what is past is past and what is present is happening right now. The only thing we can change is the future.

Are you looking ahead at the pleasures to be gained and the steps required to get there? Are you designing positive outcomes into your life?

Be
Optimistic

Opportunity
in Disguise

When you think of change, do you think of opportunity? Do you see an endless list of possibilities for improvement? Do you see a future that is better than the present, a vision that inspires you to leave the status quo behind? Do you embrace "kaizen," a commitment to continuous improvement? If not, think again. These are worthy questions at a time that calls for innovation and leading edge deliverables that "wow" customers. To move forward, we need opportunists, people who open their minds to positive solutions and creative alternatives. To compete, we need people who can find silver-linings in any outcome, turning mistakes into lessons and losses into gains.

Stop and think about some of the world's greatest inventions. Many were accidents, opportunities in disguise. The only reason they ultimately proved to be valuable was because the opportunists never gave up. They refused to see "undesired" outcomes as failures. These "results" were not the intended out-comes. Every attempt brought new knowledge and insight into the picture. Every attempt had something positive attached to it. The only real failure would have been the inability to find a gain.

Do you recognize opportunities in disguise?
Are you opening your mind to the endless possibilities
in your presence?

If it isn't change that people seem to resist, then what is it? Why is it that when we want to do something different, we are met with such resistance?

People are essentially motivated by two things: pain and pleasure. In other words, we seek to avoid pain and gain pleasure. This is where perception comes in, the underlying "picture" that drives human attitudes and behavior. The effective change agent understands that what one person perceives as pleasure may be viewed as pain by someone else.

As a simple illustration, consider exercise. Some people see "working out" as positive, a healthy way to relieve stress or stay fit. Others perceive it negatively, an activity that causes discomfort and pain. These "pictures" give people reason to pursue an activity, or resist it. Thus, if you are trying to "make a difference" or lead a change that you perceive as positive, it is this perception that you must sell. Until others see the benefits that you see (or the pain associated with staying the same), you are likely to be met with resistance.

Remember, it is not change that people resist. It is their perception of the change that motivates their response. Effective leadership requires tuning into the perceptions people have – of you, of your ideas, of your vision, and of the actions you want to implement. Learn to sell positive perceptions and you learn to sell change.

Are you projecting the positive aspects of change?
Do those around you share your positive perceptions?

The
Power of
Perception

Ask "Why?"

In an age of standard operating procedures, policy manuals and ISO-9000 audits, people often lose sight of the reasoning behind the actions, – the "why we do what we do" factor. From Fortune 100 companies to small, entrepreneurial ventures, we find people focusing more on how to complete a task rather than why the task is important. In some cases, we find people doing unimportant, irrelevant things really well.

Looking ahead, this kind of mindless waste cannot be tolerated. While standards and procedures serve a valuable purpose, they are temporary in nature. People at every level in every organization must recognize that what works today may become obsolete tomorrow due to raised standards and revised procedures. There would be little value today in being recognized as the world's most efficient 8-track tape producer.

To facilitate the ongoing change process, people need to be encouraged to ask why, as annoying as the question may seem. The question why is intuitive in nature, searching for meaning and purpose. It promotes thinking at a deeper level, challenging people to question assumptions and paradigms that often limit our outcomes. By asking why, we discover waste and uncover opportunity for improvement.

Do you know the ultimate reason why you are doing what you do? Are you remembering to ask, "why?"

The word "entrepreneur" means undertaker. Entrepreneurs undertake risk to turn ideas into results. They are not afraid to take chances, to go where others dare not tread. To think like an entrepreneur, you have to accept ownership and take responsibility for your ideas and the results you hope to achieve. You have to recognize that you are in the driver's seat. You are the one who has to make the first move.

The "dependency syndrome," that seemingly safe and secure posture where people depend on the hierarchy for stability and direction, is crippling great organizations. The new era calls for people who are self-directed, self-disciplined leaders, people who know their purpose and pursue it with ownership, passion and accountability.

Thinking like an entrepreneur means acting like you own the place. It means wearing whatever hats are necessary to add value and deliver results. It means identifying niche opportunities, pulling together virtual teams and tapping resources others seem to ignore. Look into the heart, mind and soul of an entrepreneur and witness the very characteristics required in today's environment – imagination, spirit, courage, conviction, tenacity, responsibility and resourcefulness. Then look in the mirror. Are you thinking like an entrepreneur?

Are you willing to take risks? Do those who know you best describe you as resourceful, self-directed and passionate?

Think
Like an
Entrepreneur

Be Resourceful

What if your "job description" read something like this: Know your purpose. Dazzle your customers. Be a team player. Meet your deadlines. Expand your skills. Share your knowledge. Be honest. Seek continuous improvement. Benchmark. And think change. Would you know what to do? Better yet, what if you had no job description or boss at all? Could you figure out what to do, how to do it, and when to do it?

You are far more resourceful than you might think. When faced with crises and uncertainty, positive people have an amazing ability to "make the best of things," to "pull together" and "find solutions." All it takes is a positive attitude and a genuine belief in oneself. We see it among families who have lost everything due to natural disasters. We see it among nations suffering from physical, financial and civil turmoil. And we see it among individuals who have lost jobs, income, health or loved ones. Somehow, positive people come out stronger, gaining from the experience.

Being "resourceful" means knowing how to find answers. It means being proactive, asking the right questions, reading the right books, adapting to unexpected circumstances and solving problems. It means confronting fear and insecurity, thus gaining strength and self-esteem. We may not be able to avoid life's moments of uncertainty and adversity, and we may never learn to embrace them, but we can deal with them. We can summon the courage and the strength to move on. We can be positive and resourceful.

Could you make great things happen without being told exactly what to do and how to do it?

Historically, most businesses have been set up to operate like baseball teams. Everyone has a certain amount of "turf" to cover with the game being "sequential" in nature. You do your thing and then lob the ball over to me so I can do mine. We have created "silos," often called departments, separating processes into functions. We have written job descriptions that are narrow in focus and emphasize functional expertise. This makes things easier on employees because it allows them to master and repeat one task. There is only one problem with this line of thinking, this traditional paradigm. It's too slow.

Today's competitive atmosphere calls for speed, innovation and teamwork. To be successful, people have to see beyond their narrow, rote job descriptions. They have to commit to lifelong learning, focusing on the "big picture" and the "connections" between functions. It's not enough to have efficient functions. To win in today's world, we need efficient processes. We need employees who get excited about learning multiple tasks through cross-training and teamwork, ultimately closing the inefficient "gaps" between functions. We need people who want to understand and "own" the entire process.

This new business culture resembles a basketball game, a fast, dynamic atmosphere where players have to cover for one another on a moment's notice. The players still have positions and the game still has structure, but each player adapts quickly to the dynamic nature of the game, taking ownership for whatever is necessary to advance the team. There is no room for a "That's not my job" mind-set. Winning teams think change. Anything else means falling behind.

Are you focused on the big picture, or your own narrow "silo?" Are you willing to quickly adapt to help your team?

Cross-train for Success

Exercise Your Intuition

As human beings, we are blessed with some extraordinary gifts: the ability to dream, to imagine, to conceptualize, to visualize and to create. Our intuition enables us to see patterns and make connections, empowering us to solve problems rationally and intelligently. All we have to do is practice using it.

This is where we often defeat ourselves. Given the fact that we live in a "left-brained," realistic, matter-of-fact society, people frequently ignore their "right-brained," abstract, creative side. We are encouraged to ask *how*, not *why*. We are conditioned to see things "as they are," not "as they could be." We are told to focus on the immediate, not the future, and to trust the facts, not our instincts.

This presents a great challenge to people. As customer expectations rise and new forms of competition appear, there is an increasing demand for creativity and innovation in the workplace. Now more than ever, we need to embrace and exercise our intuitive abilities. We need to ask "what if" and "why not" on a regular basis. We need to consider three solutions for every problem and use metaphors to find connections. We need to step back and look at circumstances from multiple points of view, using reverse questions to stimulate ideas and provoke "out of the box" suggestions. We need to write business plans using thoughtful, comprehensive narrative. This is how we exercise our intuition. This is how we tap into the extraordinary gifts so many people are leaving behind.

Are you ready to work at seeing things "as they could be" instead of simply "as they are?" Are you willing to start exercising your creativity?

Satisfying customers no longer assures customer loyalty and retention. Not today, and not in the future. Customers these days expect more than mere satisfaction. They want to be "wowed." They want to experience excellence on two critical axes, the combination of which leads to customer loyalty and, ultimately, customer advocacy.

The first axis, the more traditional measure, addresses "outcome." Here, customers are increasingly expecting more than the predetermined objective. They want extras. They want value-added. They want something that goes beyond expectations, something that leaves them pleasantly surprised. Simply meeting customer expectations in terms of outcome is now considered standard. It may satisfy them. But it will not inspire them to remain loyal or to tell the world how great you are.

The second axis measures "process," the ease factor. In other words, how easy is it to get the outcome? Do I have to jump through ten hoops and wait three days to get something done that takes an hour? Or do I walk away astonished by the incredibly positive experience I just had, finding myself compelled to spread the word?

Are you "wowing" your customers by going beyond normal standards? Are your customers raving about you to others?

Redefine Standards

Benchmark Your Goals and Processes

Imagine setting a goal to accelerate a process by twenty-percent next year. Sounds reasonably impressive, doesn't it? Now imagine meeting with a company that is already doing a similar process 300% faster than your stated goal. Changes your perception a bit, doesn't it? Suddenly, you see a need to rethink your plans, maybe sharpen your focus a little.

Now consider your plan of attack had you not benchmarked this process with another company. How competitive would your goal be? How effective would your planning be?

Benchmarking is not industrial tourism. It is not a one-time visit to the plant down the street or a field-trip to a convention. It is a deliberate, team-oriented process focusing on a specific product, service or method you want to improve. It is a "partnering" process with proven leaders, inside and outside your industry. It is a process requiring commitment, trust and respect.

Benchmarking is quickly becoming one of the most vital management practices in modern times. By using a continuous, systematic process for evaluating best practices among leading organizations, you gain tremendous insight and ideas on how to compete more effectively. You raise the bar. You challenge assumptions. You change beliefs. You see the impossible become possible. You find yourself saying "Wow!"

How do you know if your current goals will result in making you more competitive? Is benchmarking a practice you regularly employ?

As more and more businesses are searching for ways to inspire their employees and "wow" their customers, a new form of competition is emerging. This new form of competition is any company your people come in contact with in a positive way. In other words, if your customers are experiencing "Disney friendliness" or "FedEx speed," they are likely to start wondering, either consciously or subconsciously, why you are not doing the same. Why can't you be more responsive and friendly? Why can't you answer the phone on the first ring? Why can't you get the order here tomorrow?

The same questions will arise with your employees. As information about other great employers becomes more available, they start wondering why you are not more competitive. Why don't you have a more inspiring culture? Why aren't you building employee esteem? Why don't you provide better training? Why don't you have cross-functional teams in place? Why aren't you sharing the wealth? Why aren't you a "preferred" employer?

These comparisons, whether rational or not, are being made as leading organizations are touching more and more people. It may not seem fair, but it is real and it is happening now.

Are you benchmarking your organization against the best in the world? Do your employees and customers view you as "one of the best?"

The World
is Your
Competition

Advocate Excellence

In the past, it was common practice to define an industry leader by size and marketshare. The emphasis was on big. In automotive, this meant General Motors was king. In computer hardware, it meant IBM led the pack. In retail, Sears ruled until Wal-Mart raced by. The list goes on. General Electric. AT&T. Boeing. Kodak.

Today, a new definition of industry leader is emerging, although it is rarely articulated. This new definition describes the leader as the one "setting the standards," the company on the leading edge, the high performance enterprise forcing everyone else to play "catch up." It may or may not be the biggest in the industry, but it is undeniably the best. It is the benchmark. It is the innovator, the one with the most productive, efficient, effective systems. It is the company with the highest percentage of customer advocates.

As an illustration, consider Lexus, a division of Toyota. Years ago, when Lexus first came on the market, the company experienced a need to recall some of its cars. Recognizing the inconvenience (i.e. process) of a recall, as well as the problem to be fixed (i.e. outcome), Lexus picked up the car, repaired it, washed it, filled it with gas, and returned it with a gift on the front seat. The company turned a problem into an opportunity. It found a way to exceed, and thereby, elevate the existing standard, forcing other luxury car companies to react. It took the lead, seeking a creative and proactive way to differentiate itself from everyone else. It thought change.

Is your organization setting new standards for excellence? Are you thinking of creative ways to distinguish yourself from the pack?

One way to begin distinguishing yourself from the pack is to tap into technology. As an example, consider this book. With the introduction and advancement of laptops, word processing software, fax machines and e-mail capability, the amount of time required to write, edit, revise, transfer, design and print a book is cut significantly. In fact, I find it hard to imagine using a typewriter anymore, let alone paper and pencil, to accomplish this task.

Of course, capitalizing on the rapid advancement of technology requires a genuine commitment to lifelong learning. Fearing a new computer or an upgrade in software is not a wise choice. We have to keep up. We have to think change. We have to educate ourselves on these tools, recognizing that hanging on to "old ways" is a subtle form of waste. Time is what life is all about. We can use it wisely, tapping into technology to "free" ourselves from current constraints, or we can use it inefficiently, locking ourselves into comfort zones that limit our resourcefulness and effectiveness.

Stop and look around. Consider the awesome advancements in farming, housing, communication, entertainment, travel, manufacturing, computers, safety and health care. Where would we be today without these improvements?

What will your future hold if you choose not to keep up? Are you willing to work at keeping up with technology?

Tap Into Technology

Think
Lean

One of the most profound shifts in organizational thinking today is the shift from "push" management to "pull" management, particularly in manufacturing and retail. In days past, it was common practice to build large inventories, assuming economies of scale, and then push those products into the marketplace, often using discounts and incentives to sell them faster. Few companies in the United States recognized that the cost of maintaining these giant inventories was extraordinary. Others didn't care. They simply passed the costs on to the consumer.

Pull management is a shift in assumptions, driven by relentless pressures to simultaneously improve quality, increase speed, reduce costs and deliver value. Using a pull approach, product is not manufactured until there is an order for it, and it is not started until it can be finished. In other words, there is virtually no "excess" in the system and costs are reduced as a result. Notice this the next time you are in the checkout lane at the grocery store. As the attendant scans the products, calculating the payment required, the computer is simultaneously reordering the products, keeping a lean, steady supply on hand.

Applying the lean concept has led many companies to discover that they have more space and more capacity than previously believed. What was once an overcrowded, cramped operation with piles of "in-process" inventory and outdated clutter is now a lean, organized cycle where teams "attach" themselves to orders from start to finish. With lean thinking, quality improves, speed increases and costs are reduced, generating huge gains in productivity and profitability.

Are you learning to do more with less?

Are you thinking lean?

Two powerful forces are leading many organizations into a more adhoc, or temporary, environment. The first is a movement from an internal, management-driven focus to an external, customer-driven focus. The second is a movement from a stable, control-oriented mindset to a more flexible, adaptive mind-set. These two forces combined create the adhocracy, the opposite of the hierarchy. Driving the adhocracy is the need for speed, customer responsiveness and "out-of-the-box" thinking.

Where the hierarchy calls for rules, regulations and structure, the adhocracy seeks spontaneity, innovation and entrepreneurial spirit. Where the hierarchy emphasizes positions and functional titles, the adhocracy emphasizes assignments and cross-functional teams. These differences are extraordinary and adjusting to this new climate is challenging for most people. In other words, the thought of becoming an "entrepreneur" after thirty years in the hierarchy is painful.

The good news is that this is not an "all or nothing" transition. Hierarchy is good and it will always be good when managed effectively. Every organization has a need for efficient systems, organization and structure. The key is to recognize that hierarchy is secondary to purpose. We do not work for the hierarchy. We work for a higher purpose, a reason that goes beyond our job title. It is with this purpose in mind that we have to adapt, innovate and do whatever it takes to excel. Thriving in the adhocracy means going "outside the box" to create and sustain competitive advantages. It means thinking like an entrepreneur.

Are your decisions "management-driven" or "customer-driven?" Is your organization a flexible, adaptive one?

Thrive
in the
Adhocracy

Embrace Virtual Employment

Imagine being asked to leave your current "position" to lead a project team in another area. The project is expected to last twelve months and you may or may not return to your previous job. How does this strike you? Are you positive and excited about the opportunity and the possibilities that await you? Or are you leery and skeptical about "losing" your job, a job you are familiar and comfortable with? Now ask yourself, what will it take for this type of transition to happen easily and seamlessly? Consider not only your own skills and confidence level, but the skills and esteem of those you work with.

Welcome to the world of virtual employment, a natural result of the adhocracy culture. In this world, people are constantly learning and growing, preparing themselves and others for spontaneous and flexible shifts in responsibility and authority. One day you are managing a department, the next day you are running the plant while your boss is overseas working on a joint venture. One day you know everyone you work with. The next day you are being introduced to strangers. One day you are applying skills you have mastered for years. The next day you are being challenged to learn new skills. At first, you wonder when things are going to "get back to normal." Then a new assignment involving a new product for a new customer reminds you...this is normal. Get used to it.

Do changes in your responsibilities frighten or energize you? Have you embraced the world of virtual employment?

Of all of the critical change "issues" addressed in this book, "Reprogramming Beliefs" is the one I happen to believe is most important. In the end, people become that which they sincerely believe they will become. For many, this is simply a narrow, "aged" reproduction of who they are today. Why? Because they don't believe things can be any different. They never expand their horizons. They never put themselves to the test. They fail to use change to their advantage, resisting it rather than embracing it. Their inner voice is telling them to be wary, skeptical and distrusting. Instead of hearing a nurturing voice of confidence and support, they go through life hearing "you can't do this" and "you shouldn't do that."

If your inner voice is not your greatest fan, then "reprogram" it. Tune out the old static and listen to something new. Challenge your assumptions about yourself, your potential and your future. Exercise your intuition and your resourcefulness. Identify and study role models, people already doing what you want to do. Learn from the experts. Confront your fears. Just do it! Life is too short, and changing too fast, to listen to negative self-talk and destructive criticism. You are who you believe you are. Change your beliefs and you will change your outcomes.

Will you settle for a future that is simply an "aged" version of the present? Are you resisting change or embracing it?

Reprogram Your Beliefs

Benefit from CHANGE

Some people say that the worst thing we can wish is that nothing ever changes. I believe this is true. Without change we limit ourselves – physically, mentally, emotionally and spiritually. We sit idle, giving nothing and gaining nothing.

The root word for "motivation" means movement, and movement is change. Stop and think about it. Are you moving forward, or standing still? Are you putting your mind, energy and resources into benefiting from change, or are you fighting it?

Effective people benefit by giving to others. They add value. They fill needs. They solve problems. They help people. They are on the move, making a difference and cherishing the fact that change is a gift to humankind. It is something we need. It gives us wisdom, strength and stimulation, challenging us to reach new heights.

Choose change, and make a difference in life!

John Murphy is a highly recognized author, speaker and management consultant. Drawing on a diverse collection of team experiences as a corporate manager, consultant, and collegiate quarterback, John has appeared on over 400 radio and television stations and his work has been featured in over 50 newspapers nationwide.

As founder and president of Venture Management Consultants, John specializes in creating high performance work environments. Among the organizations he has provided services to are AT&T, American Express, AlliedSignal, Chase, Hilton Hotels, Prudential Securities, the Michigan State Senate, The New York Times, Target Stores and the CIA. Prior to consulting, John served as corporate director of human resources for Paulstra CRC, an international automotive division of Hutchinson SA in Paris, France.

John is a graduate of the University of Notre Dame and the Human Resource Executive Program at the University of Michigan, and now lives in Grand Rapids, Michigan, with his wife, Stephanie, and their four children.

His other books include:

- Agent of Change:
  Leading A Cultural Revolution
- Reinvent Yourself:
  A Lesson In Personal Leadership
- Get A Real Life:
  A Lesson In Personal Empowerment
- The Eight Disciplines:
  An Enticing Look Into Your Personality
- Pulling Together:
  The 17 Principles of Effective Teamwork

For more information, contact:

Venture Management Consultants, Inc.
PO Box 6651,
Grand Rapids, MI 49516
Phone (800) 942-1120
Fax (616) 942-2122
E-mail: jmurphy@iserv.net

The cost is low...
but the ideas are priceless!

Share these books with your entire organization and watch the power of your team grow!

Each title in the Successories "Power of One" library takes less than 30 minutes to read, but the wisdom they contain will last a lifetime. Take advantage of volume pricing as you share these insights with all the people who impact your career, your business and your life.

Anatomy of A Leader
Carl Mays
This body of knowledge can help everyone develop the qualities of a leader. #NF713259

Attitude: Your Internal Compass
Denis Waitley and Boyd Matheson
These practical insights will help managers and employees maintain a positive outlook each day. #NF713193

Burn Brightly Without Burning Out
Dick Biggs
Boost morale and productivity by helping people balance the work they do with the life they lead. #NF716016

Companies Don't Succeed... People Do
Mac Anderson
Learn to develop employees and a recognition culture within any organization. #NF716015

Dare to Soar
Byrd Baggett
The spirit of eagles inspired this unique collection of motivational thoughts. #NF716006

The Employee Connection
Jim Harris
Learn to empower your people through open communication with these valuable tips. #NF716018

Empowerment
Ken Blanchard and Susan Fowler Woodring
Use these valuable ideas to achieve "Peak Performance Through Self-Leadership." #NF716022

Fall In Love with Your Future
Ron and Mary Beshear
Apply the principles outlined in this refreshing book and begin to take control of your future. #NF716026

Goals
Gary Ryan Blair
A refreshing mix of insights and thought-provoking exercises make this a "Guideline for Designing an Extraordinary Life." #NF716025

Ignite Your Creative Spark
Jordan Ayan
This book will reveal your hidden potential as it inspires new vistas of creative exploration. #NF716023

Motivating Today's Employees
Bob Nelson
Use this book to understand the impact of employee rewards and recognition. #NF716007

Motivating Yourself
Mac Anderson
This unique mix of proven ideas and motivating stories will help "Recharge the Human Battery." #NF716021

Motivation, Lombardi Style
Vince Lombardi
Inspire your team with these insights about the athletic playing field and the business battlefield. #NF716013

Priorities
Peggy Anderson
Learn about what it takes to "Make a Difference in the Life of a Child" and share it with others. #NF716027

The Psychology of Winning for the 21st Century
Dr. Denis Waitley
Dr. Denis Waitley provides a unique perspective on what it means to win in the 21st Century. #NF716024

Pulling Together
John Murphy
Share "The 17 Principles of Effective Teamwork" with every member of any team. #NF716019

Quality, Service, Teamwork
This valuable resource includes over 100 motivational quotes on various topics. #NF716014

Results
Jeff Blackman
Help your sales team turn passion into profit with these "Proven Strategies for Changing Times." #NF716017

Rule #One
C. Leslie Charles
There are common sense tips and easy-to-apply rules in this customer service handbook. #NF716008

Teamwork
Glenn Parker
This is a valuable blueprint for successful team building. Put it to work for your team. #NF716012

Think Change
John Murphy
This provocative commentary is designed to change people's thinking—"To Adapt and Thrive or Fall Behind." #NF716020

We've Got to Start Meeting Like This
Ron Fry
Learn to reach for results and get more out of your team meetings with these insightful tips. #NF716028

Everything You Need to Know to Get Everything You Want
Robert Stuberg
Your view of yourself and the world around you will change as you discover and apply these "Life Secrets for Success." #NF716029

Heartpower
Jim Harris, Ph.D.
This valuable advice is intended to "Get Your People to Love Your Company." #NF716030